My Totems are My Best Friends

By Ellen Ronson

Illustrated by Natia Warda

Library For All Ltd.

In the Torres Strait Island culture, we have totem animals. My family's totem is the *umay* (dog).

I live with my dogs on Thursday Island, right at the tip of Australia.

3

My two dogs, Bella and Shiney, are my best friends.

They are loyal, happy, trusting and fun — just like our family.

On the island, our family is well known for having a doggy daycare.

We look after many different dogs; we take them for walks on the beach.

"It's a sunny day," I said. "Aka, can we take the dogs for a walk and a swim on the beach?"

"Yes, let's take them," replied Aka, my grandmother. "But, Frankie, you will have to wash them when we come back. I don't want them to make the house dirty."

At the beach, Bella and Shiney bolted for the clear blue water. They kicked up the sand under their paws as they raced each other to hit the water first.

We laughed and watched them frolic in the water, splashing each other.

I went into the water with the dogs, too.

Bella spotted a school of tiny fish. She tried to snap at them and catch them in her mouth.

Looking back at me playing in the shallow water, she watched me like a mother would.

Then, she froze as she saw something in the water near me...

A shark!

Bella bolted towards me. She grabbed my clothes and began to drag me to shore.

I started laughing — thinking it was a game — until I saw the fin of the shark swimming away, back out into the deep water.

We made it to the shore.

Shiney came to see if I was alright and licked me all over.

What loyal friends they were!

After that, both dogs continued to play. They rubbed their backs into the sand and got very dirty.

"Time to go, Frankie!" yelled Aka.

Shiney and Bella followed along beside us as we walked home.

Aka took Shiny to bathe her. She loved the water and getting a good clean and massage from the soap.

Bella, on the other hand, didn't like baths at all.

I had to give Bella a treat and tie her to the tree as I went to get the hose. She barked as she saw the hose, but couldn't go anywhere.

After hosing her down, I went to set her free. She shook water all over me!

I was saturated! I laughed as I chased her around the yard for being a cheeky girl.

Aka heard my laughter and let Shiney join in on the fun.

Soon, my mum pulled up in the driveway. She had some treats for the dogs.

They raced over with excitement, ready to do anything for food.

I love my dogs; they are so special.

We have so much fun together.

WASHING A DOG

1. Tie your dog up, so they can't run away.

2. Use the hose or tap to wet your dog's fur all over. Careful to not wet their eyes and ears.

3. Lather the soap on your hands and massage the dog's back, legs and under their belly.

4. Make sure the dog has soap all over them and massage them.

5. Next, use the water to thoroughly rinse off all the soap suds.

6. Lastly, grab a towel to dry off your dog. Then, unclick the leash, letting them free to shake off the rest of the water by themselves.

You can use these questions to talk about this book with your family, friends and teachers.

What did you learn from this book?

Describe this book in one word. Funny? Scary? Colourful? Interesting?

How did this book make you feel when you finished reading it?

What was your favourite part of this book?

About the author

Ellen Ronson was born on Thursday Island and is part of the Kala Lagaw Ya language group, with connections to Badu and Coconut islands. She loves spending quality time with her family and grandchildren. Her favourite story as a child was *Noni Fruit Story*.

Some words from Torres Strait Creole, a language spoken on Thursday Island:

- Aka: Grandma
- Umay: Dog

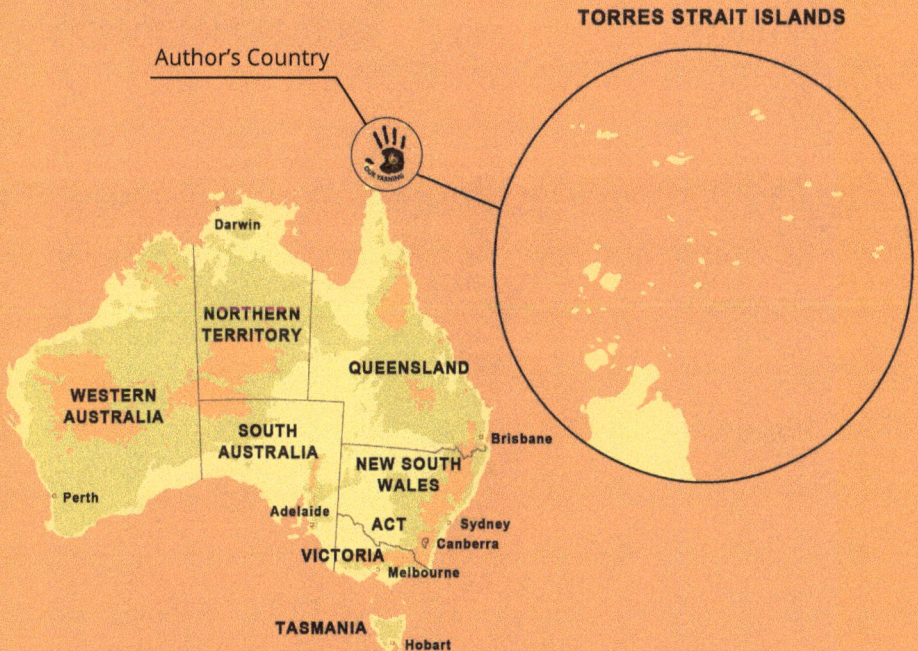

TORRES STRAIT ISLANDS

Author's Country

Darwin

NORTHERN TERRITORY

QUEENSLAND

WESTERN AUSTRALIA

SOUTH AUSTRALIA

Brisbane

NEW SOUTH WALES

Perth

Adelaide

ACT

Sydney
Canberra

VICTORIA

Melbourne

TASMANIA

Hobart

Our Yarning

The Our Yarning collection aligns with the Australian Curriculum through the Cross-Curriculum Priorities — Aboriginal and Torres Strait Islander Histories and Cultures. The collection provides an authentic opportunity for learning and embedding Aboriginal and Torres Strait Islander perspectives because it is written by Aboriginal and Torres Strait Islander people.

We know that children learn better, and enjoy reading more, when they see themselves in the stories, characters and illustrations of the books they read.

To download the app, visit the Google Play Store or Apple Store and search 'Our Yarning'.

libraryforall.org

You're reading Middle Primary

Learner – Beginner readers
Start your reading journey with short words, big ideas and plenty of pictures.

Level 1 – Rising readers
Raise your reading level with more words, simple sentences and exciting images.

Level 2 – Eager readers
Enjoy your reading time with familiar words, but complex sentences.

Level 3 – Progressing readers
Develop your reading skills with creative stories and some challenging vocabulary.

Level 4 – Fluent readers
Step up your reading skills with playful narratives, new words and fun facts.

Middle Primary – Curious readers
Discover your world through science and stories.

Upper Primary – Adventurous readers
Explore your world through science and stories.

Library For All is an Australian not for profit organisation with a mission to make knowledge accessible to all via an innovative digital library solution. Visit us at libraryforall.org

My Totems are My Best Friends

First published 2024

Published by Library For All Ltd
Email: info@libraryforall.org
URL: libraryforall.org

Our Yarning logo design by Jason Lee, Bidjipidji Art

Original illustrations by Natia Warda

My Totems are My Best Friends
Ronson, Ellen
ISBN: 978-1-923207-83-7
SKU04394